PAVILIONS IN THE AIR

空中楼阁 KŌNG ZHŌNG LÓU GÉ

Chinese proverbs and their English equivalents

汉英谚语成语 HÀN YĪNG YÀN YǓ CHÉNG YǓ

Frances Wood
吴芳思

Christopher Arnander
安难得

with illustrations by
Kathryn Lamb

梁可仁　图画

Also available in this series:

You Can't Get Blood out of a Turnip (Italian)
Apricots Tomorrow (Arabic)
The Son of a Duck is a Floater (Arabic)
Unload Your Own Donkey (Arabic)

PAVILIONS IN THE AIR

Stacey International
128 Kensington Church Street
London W8 4BH
Tel: +44 (0)20 7221 7166; Fax: +44 (0)20 7729 9288
www.stacey-international.co.uk

© Frances Wood & Christopher Arnander 2008
© Illustrations Kathryn Lamb

ISBN 978-190529-96-76
2 4 6 8 0 9 7 5 3 1

British Library Cataloguing-in-Publication Data
A catalogue record for this publication is available from the British Library

Printed and bound in Singapore

AUTHORS' PREFACE

'A proverb is the horse of conversation,' say the Yoruba, while the *Oxford Dictionary of Proverbs* refers to their ability 'to provide the sauce to relish the meat of ordinary speech.' On the other hand, Lord Chesterfield called proverbs 'the rhetoric of the vulgar man'. Whether one views proverbs as common platitudes or the spice of language, we all use them all the time. They are a linguistic phenomenon of global proportions; and nowhere are proverbs more prevalent than in China.

Chinese proverbs stem from China's long history. Many derive from the oral tradition of China's peasants, but others come from ancient classics, such as Confucius' observation that a good workman always keeps his tools in good order or the great Taoist thinker Zhuangzi's remark on the significance of experience, 'The summer cicada knows nothing of the spring or autumn'.

Many Chinese proverbs come in the form of *chengyu* or four-character phrases, reflecting the value Chinese place on concision and precision. The four-character *chengyu* themselves are sometimes shortenings of longer sayings. Similarly, English proverbs can be abbreviated; 'a stitch in time' is understood without needing to add 'saves nine'.

Apart from the philosophers of old, Chinese history is also a common source. Yue Fei, a twelfth-century general, remarked, 'If you don't tip up the gourd, you won't get the oil out', similar to being unable to 'make an omelette without breaking eggs'; and a couplet by the eighth-century Tang poet Li Bai, 'Sadly people are never satisfied, for, having conquered the state of Long, they look longingly at the state of Shu' echoes 'the grass is always greener the other side of the fence.'

Episodes from Chinese history have themselves become legendary through their re-telling in historical novels, such as *The Romance of the Three Kingdoms* about the Warring Kingdoms of the third century, or *The Water Margin* about twelfth-century battles. From the latter come such sayings as 'without blows, one can't become friends.'

Through such re-tellings, originally real-life characters become mythic, like the third-century warrior Guan Yu becoming the God of War and worshipped in many a shrine until recent times. As the English will say 'speak of the devil' the Chinese will 'speak of the red face and along comes Duke Guan.' (Guan Yu was always depicted with a bright red face, a colour that symbolised bravery and valour.)

HH Hart, in his *Chinese Proverbs* (1937), observed that ordinary Chinese people 'may be almost said to speak largely in proverbs.' This was well understood by Mao Zedong and Deng Xiaoping, whose use of proverbs demonstrated their earthiness and identification with ordinary folk and the peasant tradition. Mao's *Little Red Book* is full of proverbs and Deng's use of a Sichuan proverb that, 'it doesn't matter whether a cat is white or black as long as it catches mice' has passed into legend.

There is not always a generally known English equivalent of a Chinese proverb, for example 'Stir the grass to alert the snake' which denotes attacking an underling to get at the boss. Conversely, there is no (exact) Chinese equivalent of 'An apple a day keeps the doctor away', a particularly Anglo-American proverb, arising out of the eating and farming habits of the USA and Britain; (a similar Chinese proverb runs 'In winter, eat turnips; in summer, eat ginger and you won't need to trouble the doctor', an abbreviated variant of which is on page 58). Proverbs naturally reflect the preoccupation of each nation. 'An ant hole can destroy a thousand-mile dyke' reflects the awesome power, for good and evil of China's mighty rivers, whereas 'A small leak will sink a great ship' testifies to England's history as a maritime nation.

We are presenting a small selection from thousands of Chinese proverbs. Our aim is to entertain, but we hope that we may be able to provide a measure of instruction as well. We welcome comments on our selection and interpretations, some of which may be open to question; we fully expect to be tarred with the brush 'Wise men make proverbs, fools repeat them'.

CA & FW

抛砖引玉

Paozhuan yinyu

Throw a brick to attract jade

To set a sprat to catch a mackerel

雪上加霜

Xuě shàng jiā shuāng

Add frost to snow

It never rains but it pours

[*Shakespeare*: When sorrows come, they come not single spies but in battalions]

空中楼阁

Kōngzhōng lóugé

Towers and pavilions in the air

Castles in the air

千金买产，八百买邻

Qianjin mai chan, babai mai lin

Spend 1,000 cash on buying property, spend 800 cash on buying [good] neighbours

We can live without friends but not without neighbours

Choose your neighbours before the house [Arabic]

强扭的瓜不甜

Qiang niu de gua, bu tian

Wrench a melon from the vine, it won't be sweet

Wait until the time is ripe

到什么山上，唱什么歌

Dào shénme shān shàng, chàng shénme gē

Whichever mountain you are on, sing the songs of that mountain

When in Rome, do as the Romans do

搬起石头，砸自己的脚

Banqi shitou, za zijide zu

Pick up a stone, only to drop it on your foot

[Used by Mao in Moscow in 1957 to illustrate the folly of the Czar of Russia and Chiang Kai-shek in resisting revolutionaries]

To shoot oneself in the foot

隔墙有耳

Gé qiáng yǒu ěr

There are ears on the other side of the wall

Walls have ears

泥胎变不成活佛

Nitai bianbucheng huo fo

A clay Buddha figure cannot become a living Buddha

You cannot make a silk purse from a sow's ear

三人成虎

San ren cheng hu

Three people become a tiger

[Based on a story of a king who was told that a man had seen a tiger in the town; he did not believe it, but did so after hearing that two others had seen one]

What everybody says must be true

英雄所见略同

Yingxiong suo jian lue tong

Heroes' experiences are much the same

Great minds think alike

狗急跳墙

Gǒu jí tiào qiáng

A dog in a panic can leap a wall

Fear lends wings

塞翁失马

Sàiwēng shī mǎ

The old gentleman lost a horse

[The old man was very unhappy when his horse ran away across the border, but later it returned, bringing another horse with it]

A blessing in disguise

和尚归寺，客归店

Heshang gui si, ke gui dian

The monk returns to his temple, the merchant returns to his shop

The cobbler sticks to his last

猪骂乌鸦黑

Zhū mǎ wūyā hēi

Pigs curse crows for being black

The pot calls the kettle black

近寺人家不重 僧

Jin si renjia bu zhong seng

People who live near a temple do not respect monks

Familiarity breeds contempt

革命不是请客吃饭

Geming bushi qingke chifan

Revolution is not a dinner party

[as Mao Zedong said, adding that neither was it a piece of embroidery]

You cannot make an omelette without breaking eggs

不管白猫黑猫，会捉老鼠就是好猫

Bùguǎn báimāo hēimāo, huì zhuō lǎoshǔ jiùshì hǎo māo

It doesn't matter whether a cat is white or black, as long as it catches mice

[A proverb from his home province of Sichuan, referred to by Deng Xiaoping in 1962 and used against him in a campaign of 1975-76, for it suggested that he praised efficiency above following the correct political line.]

The end justifies the means

纸包不住火

Zhi baobuzhu huo

Paper can't smother fire

Truth will out

一人计段 二人计长

Yiren ji duan, er ren ji chang

One man's plan falls short, two men's plan is long

Two heads are better than one

河东狮吼

Hé dōng shī hǒu

The lioness roars on the east bank of the river

[From a Song dynasty poem by Su Dongpo (1037-1101) referring to a hen-pecked husband, bullied by his wife]

Husbands are in heaven whose wives scold not

19

骄兵必败

Jiao bing bi bai

Arrogant soldiers will certainly be defeated

Pride comes before a fall

一言既出，驷马难追

Yiyan ji chu, sima nan zhui

Once a word is out, a team of horses cannot overtake it

A word spoken is past recalling

牡丹虽好，全凭绿叶扶持

Mudan sui hao, quan ping luye fuchi

Though the peony is beautiful, it depends on its green leaves for support

The whole is more than the sum of the parts

[*John Milton*: They also serve who only stand and wait]

露出马脚来

Louchu majiao lai

Show the horse's hoof

To spill the beans

隔锅饭儿香

Ge guo fan'er xiang

Rice in another's cooking pot is more fragrant

The apples on the other side of the wall are the sweetest

老骥伏枥，志在千里

Laoji fu li, zhi zaiqianli

The old horse by the trough dreams of galloping a thousand miles

There's life in the old dog yet

近朱者紫近墨者黑

Jin zhu zhi zi, jin mo zhi hei

Close to vermillion, you'll turn red, close to ink, you'll turn black

If you lie down with dogs you will get up with fleas

拳不离手，曲不离口

Quan bu li shou, qu bu li kou

Hands always fists, a song always on the lips

Practice makes perfect

猫儿口中挖不出食

Maoer kouzhong wabuchu shi

You cannot retrieve food from a cat's mouth

It is water under the bridge

25

一鸟在手胜过百鸟在林

Yiniao zai shou shengguo bainiao zai lin

A bird in the hand is better than a hundred birds in the forest

A bird in the hand is worth two in the bush

打得雷大下的雨小

Dǎde léi dà, xiàde yǔ xiǎo

Loud thunder but little rain

His bark is worse than his bite

雷聲大，雨點小
LÉI SHĒNG DÀ, YǓ DIǍN XIǍO

打炮打麻雀

Dao pao da maque

Use a large gun to shoot a sparrow

Use a sledgehammer to crack a nut

一朝蛇咬，十年怕井绳

Yichao she yao, shinian pa jingsheng

Bitten by a snake one morning, he's been scared of [the well] rope for ten years

Once bitten twice shy

百艺无如一艺精

Bǎi yì wúrú yī yì jīng

A hundred tricks are not worth one well-mastered skill

Jack of all trades and master of none

人生在世无非是戏

Rénshēng zài shì wúfēi shì xì

Man's life on earth is a performance

Shakespeare: All the world's a stage

虎狼同席，各怀敌意

Hulang tongxi, ge huai diyi

Tigers and wolves may share a mat but they are still enemies

Cat and dog may kiss, yet are none the better friends

甘蔗没有两头甜

Ganzhe meiyou liangtou tian

Sugar cane cannot be sweet at both ends

Every medal has two sides

种瓜得瓜，种豆得豆

Zhong gua de gua, zhong dou de dou

If you plant gourds, you get gourds, if you plant beans, you get beans

As you sow, so you reap

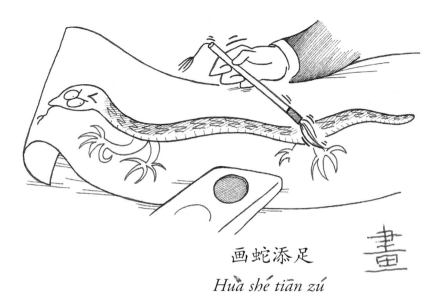

画蛇添足

Huà shé tiān zú

Add feet to a painting of a snake

Gild the lily

Shakespeare: To gild refined gold, to paint the lily…

Is wasteful and ridiculous excess

[Salisbury complains at King John's enthusiasm for a second coronation]

33

隔岸观火

Ge an guan huo

Watch a fire from the opposite bank of the river

It is easy to bear the misfortune of others

[The German word *Schadenfreude* is used as a proverb to denote taking pleasure in another's misfortunes]

天下没有不散的宴席

Tianxia meiyou bu san de yanxi

There's no banquet that doesn't end

All good things come to an end

[From the song '*There is a Tavern in the Town*':
Remember that the best of friends must part, must part]

纸笔杀人不用刀

Zhǐbǐ shā rén bù yòng dāo

Pen and brush can kill without a knife

The pen is mightier than the sword

牛不吃水，按不住头　　　頭

Niú bù chī shuǐ, àn bù zhù tóu

If the ox doesn't want to drink water, you can't hold its head down

You can lead a horse to water but you can't make it drink

滴水穿石

Dīshuǐ chuānshí

Dripping water can pierce a stone

Constant dripping wears away the stone

乱七八糟

Luan qi ba zao

Confused seven, muddled eight

To be at sixes and sevens

狡兔三窟

Jiǎo tù sān kū

A clever hare has three entrances to its nest

Don't put all your eggs in one basket

众人拾柴，　火焰高

Zhongren shichai, huoyan gao

When there are a lot of people to gather firewood, the flames burn high

[Used by Mao to counter a proposal made in 1957 that China's population should be controlled]

Many hands make light work

会捉老鼠的猫不叫

Hui zhuo laoshu de mao bu jiao

A cat that can kill mice doesn't mew

Silence catches the mouse

盲人，瞎匀　马　馬　　匀匀

Máng rén, xiā mà　YÚN

Blind man, blind horse

The blind leading the blind

[*Gospel according to St Matthew*: 'If the blind lead the blind, both shall fall into the ditch']

苏杭不到枉为人

Su Hang bu dao, wang wei ren

If you have not been to Suzhou and Hangzhou, you have wasted your life

[Two of the most famous beauty spots in China; also commemorated in sayings such as 上有天堂，下有苏杭 'Above us there is heaven, below are Suzhou and Hangzhou'.]

See Naples and die

千里送鹅毛，礼轻情义重

Qianli song emao, liqing, qingyi zhong

A goosefeather sent a thousand miles, the gift is light but the significance is heavy

Small gifts make friends, big gifts make enemies

有钱一条龙，无钱一条虫

Yǒuqián, yītiáolóng, wúqián, yītiáochóng

If you have money you are a dragon, if you don't have money, you are a worm

A man without money is no man at all

水火不留情

Shuihuo bu liuqing

Flood and fire are not merciful

The rain falls on every roof [African]

愚公移山

Yu gong yi shan

A foolish old man can move mountains

[An old man insisted that he (and his descendants) would eventually move two great peaks, if they moved a stone a day. Mao used the story to urge the masses to get rid of feudalism and imperialism through unceasing work]

Every little helps

老鸹窝里出凤凰

Laogua wo li chu fenghuang

A phoenix may emerge from a crow's nest

There's many a good cock come out of a tattered bag

[reference to the illegal sport of cock-fighting]

45

骑虎难下　　騎虎難下

Qíhǔ nànxià

When you are riding a tiger, it is difficult to get off

He who rides a tiger is afraid to dismount

树高千丈，叶落归根

Shù gāo qiānzhàng, luo ye guī gēn

The tree may grow a thousand feet tall but falling leaves return to their roots

[The second half on its own expresses the yearning for the ancestral village felt by all Chinese;
used in the title of Adeline Yen Mah's book, *Falling Leaves: the true story of an unwanted Chinese daughter*]

East west, home's best

经手三分肥

Jingshou sanfen fei

When goods pass through your hands, you can grease your palm with 30 per cent

The king's cheese goes half away in parings

九死一生

Jiŭ sĭ yī shēng

Nine deaths in one lifetime

A cat has nine lives

削足适 履

Xūezú shìlŭ

Cut away at your foot to reshape it to fit new shoes

Putting a quart into a pint pot

起马看花

Qǐ mǎ kǎn huā

Looking at flowers from horseback

[dealing superficially with a subject]

Scratching the surface

掩耳盗铃

Yăn ěr dào líng

Cover your ears to steal a bell

The cat shuts its eyes while it steals the cream

小鬼跌金刚

Xiaogui die jingang

A small devil can overturn a guardian warrior in a Buddhist temple

A David can topple a Goliath

雪里送炭

Xuěli song tàn

Send charcoal in a snow storm

A friend in need is a friend indeed

画饼充饥

Huà bǐng, chōng jī

Draw cakes to appease hunger

The wish is father to the thought

[There is a story in *The Arabian Nights* of a rich man, Barmecide, who welcomed a beggar to dinner; delicious dishes of imaginary food were served which they pretended to eat and enjoy]

狗不嫌家贫，人不嫌地薄

Gou bu xian jia pin, ren bu xian di bao

A dog doesn't notice that his household is poor, a man doesn't complain that his soil is poor

Be it ever so humble there's no place like home

公道时间唯白发

Gongdao shijian wei baifa

In the world, only [the certainty of] white hair is impartial

Death is the great leveller

枪打出头鸟

Qiang da chutou niao

The bird in the lead is the one that gets shot

The bigger the man, the better the mark

怕狼怕虎，别在山上住

Pa lang, pa hu, bie zai shanshang zhu

If you are afraid of wolves and tigers, don't go and live in the mountains

If you can't stand the heat, get out of the kitchen

[Quoted by US President Harry Truman to justify not running for the presidency in 1952]

三十六计，走为上策

Sanshiliu ji, zou wei shangce

Of the thirty-six stratagems, running away is the best policy

[From 孙子兵法 Sunzi's *Art of War*, a late (sixth century BC) Zhou classic of military tactics used throughout Chinese history by generals of all sorts, including Mao]

He that fights and runs away lives to fight another day

[In English, the French saying is often used 'Reculer pour mieux sauter']

不入虎穴，不得虎子

Bu ru huxue, bu de huzi

If you don't go into the tiger's den, you won't get its cubs

Nothing ventured, nothing gained

狐狸做梦，也想鸡

Huli zuo meng, ye xiang ji

Even when a fox dreams, it is still thinking of chickens

The leopard does not change his spots

干鱼不能给猫做枕头

Ganyu bu neng gei mao zuo zhentou

You can't give a cat a dried fish as a pillow

Opportunity makes the thief

How can the crows sleep soundly when the figs are ripe? [Indian]

十月萝卜小人参

Shiyue luobo xiao renshen

A turnip in October is like a small ginseng root

An apple a day keeps the doctor away

老子放屁，小子跑二里

Laozi fangpi, xiaozi pao erli

When the boss breaks wind, his followers run two miles

When the prince fiddles, his subjects must dance

一山不容二虎

Yi shan burong er hu

One mountain cannot contain two tigers

Two cocks cannot be on one dunghill [Turkish]

[When President de Gaulle kept UK from joining the European Common Market in 1963, a British official used this proverb to characterize his real motive]

人怕出名，猪怕壮

Ren pa chuming, zhu pa zhuang

People fear fame, pigs fear fattening

Don't put your head over the parapet

兔死, 狐悲

Tù sǐ, hú bēi

When a hare dies, a fox grieves

Carrion crows bewail dead sheep, then eat them [shedding 'crocodile tears']

麻雀虽小，五脏俱全

Maque sui xiao, wuzhang juquan

Though a sparrow is small it has the five vital organs

Small is beautiful [proverb derived from title of E.F.Shumacher's book]

The fly has her spleen and the ant her gall

有钱能使鬼推磨

You qian neng shi gui tui mo

Money can persuade the devil to push your grindstone

Money makes the world go around

千金难买一笑

Qiānjīn nàn mǎi yīxiào

A thousand pieces of gold cannot buy a smile

The Beatles: Money can't buy me love

大海捞针

Dahai laozhen

Fish for needles in the sea

To seek a needle in a haystack

一损俱损，一荣俱荣

Yi sun ju sun, yi rong ju rong

Failure follows failure, success follows success

Nothing succeeds like success

亡羊补牢

Wang yang bu lao

When the sheep are gone, mend the pen

Shut the stable door after the horse has bolted

家家都有一本难念的经

Jiajia dou you yiben nannian de jing

Every family has one sutra [Buddhist text] that is difficult to read

Every family has a skeleton in the cupboard

混水摸鱼

Hunshui moyu

Groping for fish in muddy water

Fish in troubled waters

树倒，猢狲散

Shù dǎo, húsūn sǎn

When the tree falls, the monkeys scatter

Rats desert the sinking ship

萝卜白菜，各有所爱

Luóbo báicài, gè yǒu suǒ ài

Some like carrot, some like cabbage

Every man to his taste, as the man said when he kissed the cow [Scottish]

In English, the French saying is often used 'Chacun à son goût'

金无足赤，人无完人

Jin wu zuchi, ren wu wanren

No gold is absolutely pure, no person is perfect

[Used fondly by Mao, in old age, of his political rivals, who had suffered from the Cultural Revolution he had launched; perhaps he was also referring to himself]

Everyone has his faults

Horace: Even Homer nods

狐狸说教，义在投鸡

Húli shuō jiào, yi zài tóujī

The fox speaks of religion, his idea is to steal chickens

It's a blind goose that comes to the fox's sermon

70

把卧着的老虎哄起来了，自找吃亏

Ba wozhe de laohu hongqilailiao, zi zhao chi kui

Who wakes a sleeping tiger endangers himself

Let sleeping dogs lie

Don't stroke the whiskers of a sleeping tiger [Vietnamese]

千里之堤，溃于蚁穴

Qiānlǐ zhī dī, kuì yú yǐxué

A thousand-mile dyke can be destroyed by an ant hole

A small leak will sink a great ship

To lose the ship for a ha'p'worth of tar

死知府不如一个活老鼠

Si zhifu bu ru yige huo laoshu

A dead government official is not worth as much as a live rat

A live dog is better than a dead lion

美不美乡中水，亲不亲故乡人

Mei bu mei xiang zhong shui, qin bu qin, guxiang ren

Sweet or not, water from your home village, related or not, people from your home village

Home sweet home

螳螂捕蝉黄雀在后

Tanglang bu chan huangque zai hou

A mantis stalking a cicada, a golden oriole behind

From *Jonathan Swift:* Big fleas have little fleas upon their backs to bite 'em'
And little fleas have lesser fleas and so *ad infinitum*

半斤八两

Bàn jīn bā liǎng

Half a catty, eight [Chinese] ounces

Six of one and half a dozen of the other

金窝银窝，不如自家的草窝

Jinwo, yinwo, buru zijia de caowo

Gold roofs, silver roofs are not as good as the thatched roof of one's home

Home is best

哪个鱼不识水？

Neige yu bu shi shui?

What fish doesn't know what to do in the water?

Oscar Hammerstein, *Show Boat*, 1927
Fish got to swim and
Birds got to fly

鸡毛上不了天

Jimao shangbuliao tian

A chicken feather cannot ascend to heaven

[A poor person has no chance of success or advancement in life. Mao changed the negative into a positive, 鸡毛能飞上天, *a chicken feather can indeed ascend to heaven*]

Napoleon shared Mao's view: Every soldier has a field marshal's baton in his knapsack

嫁鸡随鸡，嫁狗随狗

Jia ji, sui ji, jia gou, sui gou

Marry a chicken, follow the chicken, marry a dog, follow the dog

As you make your bed, so must you lie in it

一箭双雕

Yijian shuangdiao

One arrow, two vultures

You cannot kill two birds with one stone

远水救不了近火

Yuan shui jiubuliao jin huo

Distant water can't put out a nearby fire

Water afar quencheth not fire

藏龙卧虎

Cánglóng, wòhǔ

Hidden dragons, sleeping tigers

[Of people who lie low and hide their strength]

Dark horses

指桑骂槐

Zhi sang ma huai

Point at the mulberry to revile the ash

Hit the monkey to hurt the organ-grinder

猫不急，不上树，兔不急，不咬人

Mao bu ji, bu shang shu, tu bu ji, bu yao ren

If the cat isn't frightened, it won't run up a tree,
If a rabbit isn't anxious, it won't bite people

Even a worm will turn

检了芝麻，丢了西瓜

Jianle zhima, diule xigua

Pick up a sesame seed but lose a watermelon

Miss the wood for the trees

两姑之间难为妇

Liang gu zhi jian, nan wei fu

Between two sisters-in-law, difficult to be a wife

Caught between the devil and the deep blue sea

水能载舟，已能覆舟

Shui neng zai zhou yi neng fu zhou

Water can support a boat and can also sink it

[Used of rulers and people: the people can support a ruler but can also turn against him]

Water is as dangerous as commodious

也要马儿好，也要马儿不吃草

Ye yao maer hao, ye yao maer bu chi cao

To want a good horse that doesn't eat hay

You can't have your cake and eat it too

柳暗花明

Liu an hua ming

Flowers can bloom even in the shade of the willow tree

Every cloud has a silver lining

对牛弹琴

Duiniu tanqin

Playing music to a cow

Casting pearls before swine

[Usually seen as pointless, but a favourite theme in Chinese painting is a small boy playing the flute,
sitting on a water buffalo. It is a tranquil scene which recalls the Buddhist book
'Taming the buffalo' 牧牛图 in which a wild black buffalo is gradually tamed until he
becomes a calm white buffalo, happily listening to the music]

以毒攻毒

Yǐ dú gōng dú

Attack poison with poison

Give them a dose of their own medicine

Shakespeare Fight fire with fire

[The mother of Corialanus advising him on how to tackle his enemies]

家丑 不可外扬

Jiā chǒu bù kě wài yáng

Family scandals must not be broadcast

Don't wash your dirty linen in public

狐狸不知尾巴臭

Húli bù zhī wěiba chòu

A fox doesn't know its own tail stinks

The camel never sees his own hump

不耻下问

Bu chi xia wen

There is no shame in asking inferiors

[a quotation from Confucius, used by Mao in relation to the work of Communist Party Committees]

If counsel be good, no matter who gave it

以攻为守

Yǐ gōng wèi shǒu

Use attack as defence

Attack is the best form of defence

当着矮人，别说矮话

Dangzhe ai ren, bie shuo ai hua

Do not talk about shortness in front of a short person

Name not a rope in his house that hanged himself

Basil Fawlty: Whatever you do, don't mention the war

[In the television series *Fawlty Towers*, John Cleese, portraying a hotelier, warns a waiter in the presence of German visitors]

集腋成裘

Jiye chengqiu

Fragments of fur make a coat

Many a mickle makes a muckle

耳闻不如眼见

Er wén bù rú yán jiàn

Seeing is better than hearing

A picture is worth a thousand words

巧妇难为无米之炊

Qiaofu nan wei wu mi zhi chui

Even for a skilled housewife, it is difficult to make a meal without rice

You can't make bricks without straw

过河，拆桥

Guo he, chai qiao

Cross the river then burn the bridge

Burn your bridges [or boats]

鹬蚌相争，渔翁得利

Yubang xiangzheng, yuweng deli

When the snipe and the clam fight each other, the old fisherman gets the profit

[often used by Mao about playing off his Japanese and Nationalist foes]

Two dogs strive for a bone and a third runs away with it

老虎屁股摸不得

Laohu pigu mobude

No-one dares touch a tiger's backside

He is untouchable

[Beyond criticism or other form of attack, such as Mother Teresa or Nelson Mandela; used by Mao contemptuously about officials getting too self-important]